FEAST

FEAST

POEMS

ALEXANDRA ANTONOPOULOS

atmosphere press

CONTENTS

*

*Watch! as
the cooing lips
and gums but not the purple tongue
make a meal
of every cocky bruiser shouldering
down a corridor*

*

*

I set a furious pace

broil a steak and fill a hollow belly

cross the finish line that leads into another race

*

THE LEMON

The lemon, dimpled,
mottled, molding slowly

Keeps to himself, bittering
the olive wood bowl

Collecting errant oils
Runoff from an onion

But what might happen if
he gave it all away?

PEP TALK

do
not
devise
a future do
not construct a
sandwich of manageable
size when it comes
succumb to the gravity of the sea
do not wear your water wings
open wait watch open don't
go in with a plan prepare only to be sent
off track do not go in with a plan do not go in you
will forget it all your vision your version
of events do not let
the oracle see your black disc pupils
do not give yourself away do not
go in do not go
in do
not
go

VINEGAR & SYRUP

As the fruit fly is baptized
By vinegar and syrup
So have we content and deaf
Forged our paths according

To that which cannot make us
Whole as once we were our own
Fraternal twins within ourselves
A home within our homes

Womb-like and singular
Our connection, ever waxing

Palm to palm unborn and unafraid
Demanding absence from
Objectivity now no matter what
Why can't we recall ourselves

As God's own arm
shielding Adam's eyes

THE FEAST

Ravenous midsummer, the feast in me devours you

Dandelions raise rashlike, resolved, outpacing the

Ants, all cellulose and sinew, wrapping lengthless

Limbs
       around
           around
               around

THE HOUSE WANTS TO BE HELD

Mossy and forgiving, we yield to the threshold. Assumption
nuzzles the gutter. Naps outside.

The house. Tonight, we are in it. Tonight, closer
to ash than stars, we'll count the fictions

Dissect the sequence in the vines that
overwhelm the stone. The planet

Turns and knots our hands
into a braided rug. We won't leave.

Invite the town for cakes and milky teas.
Always ask.

Oil the locks and slip the keys
under the door. Grease the floor.

The long talk. The long silence. The
fertility of the moment. The long goodbye.

There is pulp in the air. There are seeds in our teeth. The
house wants to be held. The house bleeds us of our patience.

The house wants to be fed and kissed. I want to
hold the house. Ask.

*

*Everything that happens could
change me forever
a skeleton a smile
my skin jumps the*

*Hands clap my heart
in my throat when he says this
is the day when things fall
into place*

*What ancient chord is struck
when buzzing the harmonica
lights up my birdcage chest*

*Your life will surely change
it could be
forever*

*

HOW I WISH I WERE

As whole as when I first

emerged unblinking,

slicked

with reverence, a prism

of expectant wonder, bending boundless light

Amplifying all, pushing myself out

of my own body, glowing,

fearless in the green fluorescence

Could I still be that

neon geometry

charging

and recharging, completed

by my own circuitous love?

PLEASE

let me
be the push
and pull of the tide

where your weight
goes when you're
weightless

WHAT IS GOOD FOR ONE OF US
IS GOOD FOR ALL

Wall-eyed women

Whisper, "which way?" walking

Contradictions crossed at the

Knees touching under tables

Groping in the oak tree shade tightly

Bound as flower crowns blackening the

Blameless, shaming the shorn for their shearing,

The wall-eyed women witches steeple every finger

Wallow and wail pass and chase

The eyeball — all wrong — every

Last one of their predictions

Wrong

NO BREADFRUIT

There is no breadfruit
In the bowl and what is
There is off and gamy

I have sacrificed my date-night
Dress for us to be alone
To make you think of me

As not predator
As not pulp-eater
As not the coconut

Gluck glucking all
Its milk opaque and sour
Expecting you to spill some milk for me

Unpainted I stretch unguarded unspeaking
Across two earths collapsing kingdoms
So you might know that I'm not out to get you

I ATE TWICE THE MUSHROOMS

I ate twice
the mushrooms you did
roughly wrapped in cotton
blankets face-to-facing
wrapped around your hips

Erasing our edges blending
softly spilling jugs of dark
and light cascading into dying stars
that night I stayed awake

Speaking to myself through you I felt
cicada heavy breathing like
a palm flat on my back

I'm here
I thought you might be
saying with your eyes

Closed through the
lids the gyre in my stomach
twisting I told the
hot thick summer silence

You might be
everything
I love about
existing

MUSIC FOR MACONDO

loosed and wild

      what could be

swept up in the wind,

      what could be loosed and wild, again

      *

notes like rubies like salt like slabs
of uncooked beef laid warming to

the sound of raindrops spitting through an
open window going sour on Formica
poke the silky night

kiss the street and burst
dismantling the universe incisors first

      *

purr and growl

      the heavy chord

sustains,

      the heavy chord purrs and growls, again

THE GOLDEN RATIO

There is no greed like that which greed asks of itself as I
would flip the

Golden ratio, my stomach lining out, and eat the black seed
world inside you I am

Here for the dip in your ribs, a hollow space to press an ear

I CAME TO TALK

the pitch pine
loves
      the axe

that split it

even in a heap
of its
      own bones

now set it
all on fire

now glue the
splinters back
      in place

now brushing back
my baby hairs
swallowing

the blaze
thick
      as thistles

my iris open
like
      the moon—

*

What if you hadn't called me?

*

CONCESSIONS, OR A FULL FISH
BAKED IN SALT

Flopping on his butcher's block I
am hot with a kind of poppy wine leaking
through my seams dogwood blossom white
cream pooling in my hands

They said you are the fail-safe what they do depends on

 So I a salted cod do catch

                  the latch with any

Articulating part my fingers for
example crammed up to the knuckles deep
inside the inner workings of the latch so
I may jam the jamb and keep the hinges swinging

A bloody willing mess of fish-hooked flesh but I do catch

        The latch a salted
                cod I catch the latch with any

FEEBLE EGO, DO I NOT EXIST?

Do not meditate
on the paradox
of moth wings
do not meditate at all

Ghosts drift by
the echo chamber
shapeless forms
doling out opinions
gobbling the cooling cobbler
which ghosts cannot digest

If airy, hollow bodies
could take anchor
so they might mouth
a question they would ask
what only ghosts ask
of themselves

OHMYFUCKINGGOD

Do I really have

to keep this

in?

My knife's-edge jawbone

in your atlas hands and eyes

turned upward in some holy

supplication for the guillotine

Do I
really have to keep
this in?

O, MAKEPEACE

Thackeray said it best: One loves and

one condescends to be so treated

But he did not explain

that one will always change

The fluctuating power is what kills

the never knowing if

You are the

trigger or the torso

Implicit in

the ending always

MY BONES ON YOURS

You feed me nothing once again

I pass the time discarding bits

Of undigested pear into my palm

Peeling back my

Eyelids from their sunken

sockets howling ripe but I do

Sense that you are here to gilt the

Edges of my pages, to let me rest

TO INCUBATE A STARBURST

Balanced on a waist-high picket fence I

Am pre-dawn dividing six gins into

Sixteen steaming summers wherein

I howled for nothing but to

Fold my body up into a palace garden

To incubate a distant starburst ripping free

Kernel from papery cocoon

Yes that's still what I want I think

To bring you to the ground

I cannot stretch my legs so I am taller

Lay your head in my hands over the asphalt

Over the trains and skittering rat sounds

*

*(I will not let you
into my reflection
make me see my
ruddy cheeks my Roman nose my every choice
as some perverted choice of yours I make when
you're not looking)*

*

THE TRUTH

The truth is abject terror blooms in me, something I thought
    would never

Happen and the older I get the more aversions I have the
    more squeamish

I become the idea of exposing my soft underbelly inspires a
    recoil, a retch

How we learn to be fearless only after fearlessness has been
    drawn out of us

We are told to be fearless — life demands it — after we have
    been punished for

Our brashness, our uncompromising attitudes, our high
    expectations

After those have been teased out, shaved off, how we are
    pressured to find

Them, to pick up each broken strand scattered in the wind,
    then wear them again

The ultimate gaslight — we are born perfect and whole and
    needing and wanting

Each other then shown that our wholeness is wrong then in
   our wrongness

Redeemed but only later, much later, after things have been
   taken away, after

We hide from the ones we love, after cynicism has tainted
   hope, now

A simulacrum, satisfying neither presence nor absence —
   how

Our fragility is rewarded with carelessness

I lose my breath now remembering

Every time I felt my whole shell cracking

How I feel in pieces now

How I want

To eat the world inside you, to

Plough a zipcar through a sign on 95

To send you a picture of my ass or my hands

Or the corner of my eyes, to

Shake you by the shoulders, to say

I love you, you fucking moron, I

love you, you stupid fuck, and

don't you love

me back

*

We descend, our limbs pulled to the floor, our only objective

To deconstruct Orion, to glide a finger through the silence

Inked onto our skin, the calcified creases of noise, the night

A throbbing marvel, the density of sound

*Dampened by a cotton numbness in our ears and a ringing in
our mouths*

*Two hammers in one bell, in motion without motion,
synchronous,*

Depleted, vibrating, as the lotus eater lazes, all is well

*

WE LIVE INSIDE THE
THEATREOFEACHOTHER

i fall

into your chest

face painted, mask on

counting out staccato

heartbeats in 3/4 time

it's okay if i'm a

cipher   an onion skin

thirsting for repetition

molting for a ghost

that is you and   that is me

we live inside the

theatreofeachother

repeating ecstasies

guarding buried buckshot

while you're sleeping

i try

to put my finger on it

*

This feels like a dream but it's not but it is

The night cracked into diamonds and dead leaves

I want it to be light so they can see we disappeared

*

THIS IS THE LOOP

Braided, the loop falls
Back onto itself, loosely

Interlacing fates illuminating
Like a midnight sun burning white
And black a hot
Hex blistering and blessing unrelenting but we won't
     remember

What we saw already in the still spring
Water's ripple
Returning our bodies to ourselves, offering alternatives

This has happened all before
All of this is happening

    *

What did I say that time I braided the first loop
Burnished as it slipped fast through my grip but thick
Enough to catch and latch into a sailor's knot

A knit tight enough to tempt the
Whirl of a whipping wind, to call me to

The insides of a tree, knotted, rooted through the bottom of a

Country and spread across the earth's expanse, to think back
Through my history,
To sit on a woven rug, plusher this time than the last

I am happening again before
I happened once

      *

I'm sitting here with him and he is good
Pushing back my fallen hairs with heavy hands as I pretend
    to sleep
We form a T shape on the floor

Digging my fingers deep into his woven rug I breathe into his
    skin —
Hold this in your thoughts — and silently unweave the
    threads that keep each thread in
Place
When your knees the size of
Elephants' heads are throbbing through the sheets and you
    are seventy, stuck at a 45-degree
Angle in the bed

And your manuka honey voice box has been rented out to
    stadiums with nothing left to soothe
What burns inside a brain, when that's the case
Wipe it from the bottom
Of your mug

      *

I wring the life out of this moment — the
Color and the novelty —
Exhaust its desire to return so we

May settle peaceful into linen sheets, resplendent
Naked viable unbecoming
A coffee stain reminder reminding us of nothing

*

And what could be more rotten than
the letdown?

Giving it all
away, almost

Dumping cake into a
hole

Investing in your
"future"

Witnessing your dignity
fall away in

Clumps like soaking cocoa puffs
in milk

*

ABOUT ATMOSPHERE PRESS

Atmosphere Press is an independent, full-service publisher for excellent books in all genres and for all audiences. Learn more about what we do at atmospherepress.com.

We encourage you to check out some of Atmosphere's latest releases, which are available at Amazon.com and via order from your local bookstore:

The Distance from Odessa, poetry by Carol Seitchik
How It Shone, poetry by Katherine Barham
Wind Bells, poetry in English and Tagalog by Jessica Perez Dimalibot
Meraki, poetry by Tobi-Hope Jieun Park
Impression, poetry by Charnjit Gill
Aching to be Human, poetry by Stormy Abel
Love is Blood, Love is Fabric, poetry by Mary De La Fuente
How to Hypnotize a Lobster, poetry by Kristin Rose Jutras
The Mercer Stands Burning, night poems by John Pietaro
Calls for Help, poetry by Greg T. Miraglia
Lost in the Greenwood, poetry by Ellen Roberts Young
Blessed Arrangement, poetry by Larry Levy
Lovely Dregs, poetry by Richard Sipe
Out of the Dark, poetry by William Guest
Shadow Truths, poetry by V. Rendina
A Synonym for Home, poetry by Kimberly Jarchow
The Cry of Being Born, poetry by Carol Mariano
Big Man Small Europe, poetry by Tristan Niskanen
Lucid_Malware.zip, poetry by Dylan Sonderman
The Unordering of Days, poetry by Jessica Palmer
It's Not About You, poetry by Daniel Casey
A Dream of Wide Water, poetry by Sharon Whitehill
Radical Dances of the Ferocious Kind, poetry by Tina Tru

ABOUT THE AUTHOR

Alexandra Antonopoulos is a writer and poet living in Brooklyn, New York. Her debut collection, *Feast*, was written mostly from a windowsill while trying to coax the downstairs cat inside with the ever-tempting *pspspsps*.

Follow her across all socials @ajoyantonop.

Say hello or inquire about collaborations:
ajoyantonop@gmail.com

CPSIA information can be obtained
at www.ICGtesting.com
Printed in the USA
BVHW082257200421
605388BV00008B/1175